UNLEASH YOUR
GREATNESS
Buy That House
Start That Business
Start That Non-Profit
Always Bless Others
Get That Promotion
Get That Degree
Take That course
Activate Your Greatness
Start with Vision,
Purpose, and Plan
Written by: Vernell S. Jackson-Hackett
Illustrations: Leroy Grayson
Published by: Jazzy Kitty Publications

Unleash Your Greatness

By Vernell S. Jackson-Hackett

Cover Designed by Jazzy Kitty Publications

Published by Jazzy Kitty Publications

Logo Designed by Justin Ackerman

Editor: Anelda L. Attaway

© 2024 Vernell S. Jackson-Hackett

ISBN 978-1-954425-93-4

Library of Congress Control Number: 2024902242

DEDICATION

This book is dedicated to my best friend, my confidant, my soul mate, my husband, Blaine A. Hackett, and our Son Sieki. My daughter-in-love Tanisha and my beautiful grands Simyrah, Yasmeen, Cameron, Elon, Milan, and Isaiah.

I would like to give Honor to God for my "Favorite Girl," my mother, Dorothy Jackson, and my late father, Chester Jackson.

Also, to my "Team Empowerment," my beautiful sisters and support system, Iris, Debbie, Donnie, and Theresa.

To my always there when I need him, my brother Vernon.

To all my brothers and sisters in love and my in-laws, Thank you for all the love and support.

To all my supportive friends, sister circles, church family, and everyone who has been an inspiration and support to me in my journey, I love you and thank you.

To everyone who reads and is inspired by this book, thank you not from the bottom of my heart, but with all my heart.

God Bless!

ACKNOWLEDGMENTS

BUT GOD! I must give all the Honor and all the Glory to God. Had it not been for Him on my side, I don't know where I would have been in this journey called "Life."

Thank you to my Lord and Savior, Jesus Christ.

Thank you for Your unfailing love, grace, mercy, and the gifts You've given me. Thank you for Your word that guides and directs my paths.

You deserve it, all the Glory, all the Honor, all the Praise.

I pray that this book is pleasing in Your sight as it reveals the light of You that I strive to shine in me.

Amen and Amen!

TABLE OF CONTENTS

I'm SOOO excited to finally share some of my "GREATNESS." I've been holding onto this desire to write a book for many years. So here it is, ready for you to be inspired and prayerfully to ignite you to do whatever it is you've been wanting to do and unleash it.

It's time to unleash that greatness you have been holding onto and holding in; let it be done.

Channel that greatness so you can release and manifest the desires of your heart and reach new heights, even in areas in which you are currently successful. It is time to elevate, increase, and enlarge; there's always room for more.

We all have greatness in us, and it's just waiting for us to unleash it.

ITS TIME READY SET GO!!!

I can tell you firsthand that I knew greatness was inside of me simply because God's word says, "We have different gifts according to the grace given to each of us." Romans 12:6 NIV.

So, I said to myself it's up to me to channel my gifts, execute the process and manifest them. I know it sounds good and simple, but we know anything that's great is going to come with some challenges, but that's OK. We have to believe that we have what it takes to Unleash Our Greatness. We have to have faith in Romans 12:6 and be intentional about the process to operate in our gifts.

Honestly, for me, I had to first take time to do some spiritual inventory, which is paramount for trusting and believing in my greatness, as well as being intentional about my relationship with God. I had to realize the importance of acknowledging God consistently and daily, His love, grace, mercy, and presence in my life, and the goodness He affords me, no matter what it looked like or felt like or happening in my life at a particular time.

In that realization, I also needed to trust God and His promises, along with maintaining an intimate relationship with Him, which was the foundation to build on and that my greatness would surely be unleashed. I knew this was true because it again says in His word, "I can do all things through Christ which strengtheneth me." Philippians 4:13 KJV.

As I think about where I started really operating in my gifts, it was in October of 2012 when my husband accepted a position to pastor a church. I was automatically put in a position that I, at the time, was not ready for at all. Before I knew it, I was facilitating events for the women's ministry during various times of the year, and in between, I was invited to share on various platforms. I was doing things that I said to myself, *"Where's all this coming from?"* That greatness that was inside me, God, was ordering steps for it to be unleashed without me even knowing it, or feeling prepared, or that I even had what it took to do these things.

Then again, before I knew it, I registered to attend Freedom Bible College and Seminary in October 2015. Upon completion of my course, I received my Christian Life Coach Certification. I knew that more greatness was going to be Unleashed. I also believed God was ordering more steps.

Now I'm really starting to feel like channeling my gifts even more, especially to inspire women, as I was really feeling inspired myself. So, I started to pray and ask God to increase my territory, and my desires of elevation to new heights were ignited.

My prayers for the increase were answered. In June of 2017, I hosted my first full-day Women's Conference at an outside venue. The theme of the conference was "Time For Your Next Level." To God be the Glory, it was a huge success, very well attended. Women were blessed and charged for their Next Levels. I, too, was charged for mine and now see that I Unleashed my Greatness in that season.

That conference was a turning point for me, and I said then I wanted to write a book. I felt that I had more greatness to unleash and wanted it to be in writing and to be an inspiration to me and others.

Although I had the desire to write a book, it just wasn't time. So, I channeled just operating in my gifts. However, God ordered steps for me. I attended conferences and retreats and was blessed to speak on various platforms and get knowledge and inspiration to enhance what was to come.

Keep in mind this is me talking about my greatness, but life is still happening around me. I work full-time, and I'm the wife of a pastor, mother, grandmother, devoted family encourager, and friend. But believing in God's promises, I still had my desire to operate in my gifts and continue to Unleash my greatness.

Now, I've reached a new turning point. I attended a very powerful women's summit in October of 2021, and after attending that summit, I was very inspired and the thought of writing my book kept coming to mind. Shortly after attending that summit, I received an email that was sent out in general that preparation for 2022 was underway, and they were looking for speakers. There was a link to a very lengthy, detailed application process, and yes, I applied. A few weeks after my application was received, I received and email to be interviewed by the team of the summit. A few weeks after the interview and the team's review of hundreds of applicants and several other interviews, to

God be the Glory, I was chosen to be a speaker on their Virtual Platform.

It was exciting and scary, as I had never done a workshop virtually, but there's a first time for everything, just ask me. Again, God is ordering steps for me to Unleash more Greatness.

It was an interesting process for me; however, I was very happy to complete the 30-minute virtual workshop process with the help of my husband, friends, and niece. I had a few hiccups and hurdles, but I persevered, and it was a success.

The title of the workshop was, wouldn't you know, "UNLEASH YOUR GREATNESS!"

I attended the summit in-house at the venue. However, there was an app assigned to all summit attendees, and I could see how many people viewed the workshop as well as see how it was rated. To God be the Glory, it was viewed by many and rated extremely well. That was it. I said again to myself this is my book. This workshop had awesome content and would be the perfect book to be an inspiration to everyone, not just women.

What made this more of a reason to use this workshop for my book is that I already have the "Vision," "Purpose," and now a Plan. It is my heart's desire to really share this inspiration in book form, as well as God's word says, "Take delight in the Lord, and he will give you the desires of your heart." Psalms 37:4 NIV. I had my virtual workshop saved on my phone, and one day decided to look at it again to confirm my excitement for this to be my book. After watching it to the very end, I said to myself and talked to God about it, and the rest is history.

This book will ignite and assist everyone who has a desire to tap into their greatness and unleash it. You can start that business, get that degree, write that book, take that trip, get that promotion, buy that house, help others in ways you never imagined, be successful, go after that promotion, start that non-profit, own that company, etc... the list is infinite.

So here it is: "UNLEASH YOUR GREATNESS." I believe and have done it. Once you have a Vision, Purpose, and a Plan, you're on the perfect path to accomplishing whatever your heart desires, as well as you must believe in Psalms 37:4. Lastly, this concept was shared from a conversation I was having with my friend Di in 2018, as we were in the car driving to a women's conference in Pennsylvania that was hosted by our mutual sister/friend who we both love very much, but God loved her more, as she is now being an inspiration in Heaven.

Be intentional about Unleashing your Greatness; you have what it takes; you got this; just do the work and believe in **"I can do all things through him who strengthens me." Philippians 4:13 NIV. YOU'RE A WINNER!!!!**

STAY FOCUSED ON WHATS RELEVENT

See it and Believe it!

VISION

"Call to me, and I will answer you and show you great and mighty things, which you do not know." Jeremiah 33:3 NIV

L et's start; let's be intentional about manifesting and unleashing our greatness with a Vision. Why do we need a Vision? Well, your vision, by definition, "is the ability to think about or plan the future with imagination or wisdom." Your vision is extremely important; it's where you see exactly what you want to accomplish. We use our imagination to see it, just like it's right in front of us, and we can touch it.

I visualized this book exactly how I wanted it to be and its contents, and I instantly felt inspired by my vision. I started believing that it was real and that ignited me to do what it takes to manifest it.

Your vision is paramount; it requires self-connection and self-awareness and allows us to tap into what feeling we get when we visualize our greatness. For me, when I visualized this book, I felt excited. I felt energized to do the work.

Believe it or not, how we feel and our emotions play an important role in how we get energized and empowered to get started and to believe we can do whatever it takes to achieve and go to the next level. Especially when we have a clear vision as if it's right in front of us. That's what did it for me.

Tapping into our spiritual self is key to our vision. Greatness lies in our spiritual foundation, and it charges us to go, to move the needle forward. We must connect to our thoughts so we can channel our minds in the direction it needs to go. Everything we do in alignment with our vision comes in the form of how we think. We have to break down any barriers that will hinder how we think about our vision, so we can process with an open and clear mind that corresponds with what steps we need to take in manifesting our greatness.

With our hearts and minds clear, we can focus on the direction of our vision, and we can start to execute the process and proceed with clarity. Our vision sets the tone, and it gives direction as well as it allows us to spend time using our imagination to actually get a feel for what we're striving to achieve and what that's going to look like.

When we connect with ourselves spiritually, morally, emotionally, and mentally, we clear the pathway, and again, we can proceed with even more clarity. Confidence is what we need most, and as we tap into the areas mentioned above, we allow our minds to be focused, and we make room for the confidence we need that charges us to be ready for the challenge because we know all great things come with challenges. But that's OK. We have what it takes; we are more than conquerors. Romans 8:37

Remember, our vision starts with a thought, us using our imagination, so that means we need a positive, confident mindset, and we must self-connect, be ready for the challenges, and then be ready for the WIN!!!

Self-Check on Your Vision

"Where there is no vision the people perish: but he that keepeth the law happy is he." Proverbs 29:18 KJV

Write down what you visualize when you think about the greatness you want to unleash.

_____

_____

_____

_____

_____

_____

_____

_____

_____

_____

_____

_____

_____

_____

_____

_____

_____

_____

Write down how it makes you feel.

_____

_____

_____

_____

_____

_____

_____

_____

_____

_____

_____

_____

_____

_____

_____

_____

_____

_____

_____

_____

_____

On a scale of 1-10, how confident are you in unleashing that greatness you visualized?

_____

_____

_____

_____

_____

_____

_____

_____

_____

_____

_____

_____

_____

_____

_____

_____

_____

Your Thoughts:

Channel

Your

Greatness

PURPOSE

"We have different gifts, according to the grace given to each of us." Romans 12:6 NIV

Our next step to unleashing our greatness is "Purpose." So, our purpose is the reason for which something is done or created or for which something exists. (Def Websters) The role our purpose has is very important. When we channel our greatness, we must realize and ask ourselves a few questions. Such as, How do I see myself when it comes to revealing my greatness? Does my vision align with my purpose? What do I need to do to align and correlate my vision with my purpose?

This is the execution process for our purpose, and it's very important to understand who we are, how we think, and how we see ourselves and confirm that our vision correlates to our purpose. Once we have the answers, we can start to tap into our creative abilities. We must trust the process and do the work and have fun challenging yourself so we don't get all frustrated, although we will at times, but shake it off and stay the course. When there are distractions, remember your focus has more weight than any distraction.

With that being said, you need to spend time and lots of it, channeling your inner desires, strengths, weaknesses, as well as your level of confidence. In doing so, we allow our minds to open up so we can dissect our thoughts, which helps in determining what actions we need to take for our vision and purpose to complement each other. You'll see that as you navigate strategies to unleash your greatness, sometimes they are repetitive, which is OK; it's like double-checking to make sure it's all good.

Our purpose is the preview where we see deeper layers of our vision, and it reveals what we need to do, and how we need to do it. This is where we channel building our confidence level and believing even more in our greatness. Well, start to feel secure in what we want to accomplish and strive to do it with excellence, as well as believe in Romans 12:6. Always keep some scripture in mind; it helps with confidence and keeping a positive mindset. It did it for me, that's for sure.

Moving the needle forward in our purpose is the goal. It's like setting a stage for a scene in a play; what's on the stage correlates to a specific scene, so our purpose is like that stage. We must put in place what we need to create the correlation with our vision to manifest that greatness we want to unleash. It's where we bring it to existence. I know it sounds like a lot, but it really isn't. I say this again because anything that's great will not come easy and certainly will come with its challenges. However, we have what it takes to overcome them all; we just have to invest our time, efforts, energy, patience, and, in some cases, our finances.

Most importantly, we must believe, have much faith, and pray a lot. I know this to be true because the word says, "Therefore I tell you, whatever you ask for in prayer, believe that you have received it and it will be yours." Mark 11:24 NIV.

We can easily live our lives desiring to achieve greatness, but we need to be more attentive to the areas that are paramount in order for us to be successful and in order for us to unleash greatness. Keep in mind a positive mindset, confidence, faith, and prayer can ignite those creative juices to flow, which in turn can manifest your purpose as it correlates to your vision with clarity. Count every setback as a setup for the greater and stand on Mark 11:24.

Solidify Your Purpose!

Self-Check In: Purpose

Write down your purpose and how it aligns with your vision.

Write down strategies that will help you manifest your purpose with clarity and excellence.

_____

_____

_____

_____

_____

_____

_____

_____

_____

_____

_____

_____

_____

_____

_____

_____

_____

Find a scripture to help you stay grounded in your purpose.

_____

_____

_____

_____

_____

_____

_____

_____

_____

_____

_____

_____

_____

_____

_____

_____

_____

_____

WHEEL OF GREATNESS

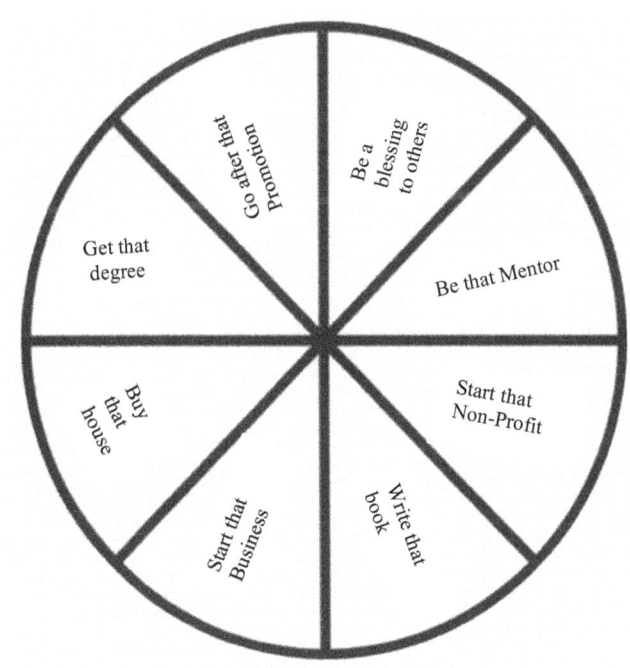

PLAN

"For I know the plans I have for you declares the Lord, plans to prosper you and not to harm you, plans to give you hope and a future." Jeremiah 29:11 NIV

The last step to unleashing our greatness is our "Plan." For clarity purposes, a plan is "A detailed proposal for doing something or achieving something." (Def Websters) Your plan reveals your "Greatness," and here you execute, activate, and achieve.

This is where the work you've done through your vision and having a purpose comes to light. Your plan unveils how you have invested in channeling what it takes to accomplish that greatness that you have desired to unleash for so long. Also, remember the inspiration of Psalms 37:4. Believe it and achieve it!

You are your best investment; I had to realize and believe that also. Once you come to this realization, you will take pride in doing the work it takes to manifest whatever your heart desires, keeping in mind that Psalms 37:4 stays at the forefront of my thoughts, giving that encouragement and assurance that I have what it takes, and God will do the rest when we think about investing in ourselves for our Plan, it's not always just about finances. For instance, it takes no money for us to invest our time, research resources that we can learn and get knowledge from, or just keep a positive mindset so we can channel in a positive direction and be focused once we can master these areas; that's half the battle.

Our plan is the finish line, so to speak, in our journey to unleash our greatness. This is where we overcame the hurdles and all that was in between to arrive at our destination. Well, feel a sense of relief in knowing that we strived to unleash and manifest with excellence.

And guess what, as we have done all the work and persevered to our greatness, it's not just for us. I know how we come to that conclusion. Well, prayerfully, we will also be inspired to help others be successful and unleash their greatness. Doing so by sharing our gifts, skill sets, talents, resources, and knowledge. It's interesting how we do all the work to accomplish and be successful, and sometimes feel like we had to do it, so now it's your turn to figure it out, but we have to remember that helping others is greatness. For me, it's an awesome feeling hearing someone say that something I said or did helped propel them to a higher level, as well it gives me confidence that I am doing what God would be pleased with. It also reminds me of my favorite scripture, "So then we pursue the things which make for peace and the building up of one another." Romans 14:19 NASB.

When we are at our Plan, it requires some of the same attention our Vision and Purpose need. There are areas we must channel, and we must maintain and balance these areas for our Plan to flourish and our greatness to show out.

It's time for a final self-check-in by tapping once again into our spiritual self, our mental space, our physical being, and, if needed, our finances because this is where it all happens.

Balance in these areas is paramount for the manifestation of our Plan. This stage of our Plan is where it's lights camera action! We have to get the balancing act down to a science. Here is where it all comes together, and we have worked very hard for this moment so we must be ready as well as believe in Philippians 4:13.

If you really think about it, you had to balance different areas throughout your vision and purpose, so by the time you reach your plan, you've had plenty of practice, so you got this!

The navigation process has been accomplished. You've taken the necessary steps to confirm that the greatness that's been inside of you is ready to be Unleashed. You started with your vision, which evolved into your purpose; you persevered through trials and tribulations by self-connecting, keeping a positive mindset, and balancing your spiritual, emotional, and physical being. You invest in yourself in ways that stretch beyond your finances, which is even more important because you gain knowledge that will always be with you forever, and with that knowledge, you can create various financial avenues for income if needed or desired. Knowledge is POWER!

I had to do all of this to get to the place I needed to be to write this book. I had to be true to my Vision, Purpose, and Plan, particularly for this book. So, my prayer is for you to do the same thing or better and for the result to be that you. **"UNLEASHED YOUR GREATNESS!"**

Self-Check In: Plan

Write down what greatness you're going to unleash.

_____

_____

_____

_____

_____

_____

_____

_____

_____

_____

_____

_____

_____

_____

_____

_____

_____

_____

_____

Write down your plan for whatever greatness you desire to unleash.

_____

_____

_____

_____

_____

_____

_____

_____

_____

_____

_____

_____

_____

_____

_____

_____

_____

Find a scripture to keep you inspired to unleash your greatness.

_____

_____

_____

_____

_____

_____

_____

_____

_____

_____

_____

_____

_____

_____

_____

_____

_____

_____

_____

_____

SUMMARY

U nleashing your greatness can be narrowed down to a Vision, Purpose, and Plan. The word of God, prayer, faith, and these 3 entities can put you on the perfect path to doing just what says, and I'll repeat it: "Therefore I tell you, whatever you ask for in prayer, believe that you have received it and it will be yours." Mark 11:24 NIV.

It's time; no more procrastinating, no more waiting for this or that to happen first, no more doubting, no more excuses, no more delays.

Take that first step and before you know it, you'll be on your way to Unleashing that greatness. Get that degree, write that book, start that business, buy that house, start that non-profit, own that company, build good relationships, go for that promotion, the list can go on infinitely.

You have what it takes; believe in, and I'll repeat it: "We have different gifts according to the grace given to each of us." Romans 12:6 KJV. Believe in and I will repeat, "I can do all things through Christ who strengthens me." Philippians 4:13: NIV.

It's been such a pleasure sharing my gift to inspire and share the greatness God afforded me to unleash. My prayer is that you are encouraged beyond measure and that you can use this book and its contents to take you to the next level. And remember your greatness is not for just you, it's for you to be an inspiration and inspire others to excel and reach new heights. So, with that being said, here's your final charge for your greatness to manifest with excellence.

Let go and let God activate your faith, believe, and **"UNLEASH YOUR GREATNESS."**

There's only one you.
And that's Special,
So, in turn,
Make you Special

BELIEVE GOD

GIVE THANKS

SPECIAL LOVE

STAY IN PEACE

KEEP A POSITIVE MINDSET

"SMILE OFTEN JUST BECAUSE"

ABOUT THE AUTHOR

V ernell S. Jackson-Hackett is a native of Wilmington, Delaware. She is devoted to serving God and has a passion for Empowering Women spiritually and motivating them to channel the gifts that God has given them so they can be an inspiration and uplift others.

Professionally, God called Vernell to healthcare at an early age; adhering to the call, she attended and graduated from Delcastle Vocational Technical High School with a diploma in Medical Assisting. After a few years of working in the medical field as a Radiology Assistant, she decided to further her education, attending and graduating from the St. Francis Hospital School of Radiologic Technology. After graduating and passing her Radiology and Mammography Boards, she has been and is currently employed by St. Francis Hospital for 37 years.

BUT GOD!

Vernell is the proud wife of Blaine A. Hackett, a mother, daughter, sister, aunt, friend, and a devoted family member who loves spending time with family, playing games, and having fun with LOTS of laughter.

Vernell has a strong desire to do and be what's pleasing to God as well as daily and consistently strives to be obedient to whatever He has for her to do, no matter what hat she is wearing.

Favorite Scripture:

"Let's pursue what leads to peace and building up one another." Romans 14:19 NASB

Life Scripture:

"I can do all things through Christ who strengthens me." Philippians 4:13

www.ingramcontent.com/pod-product-compliance
Lightning Source LLC
Chambersburg PA
CBHW051250120626
46547CB00014B/1883

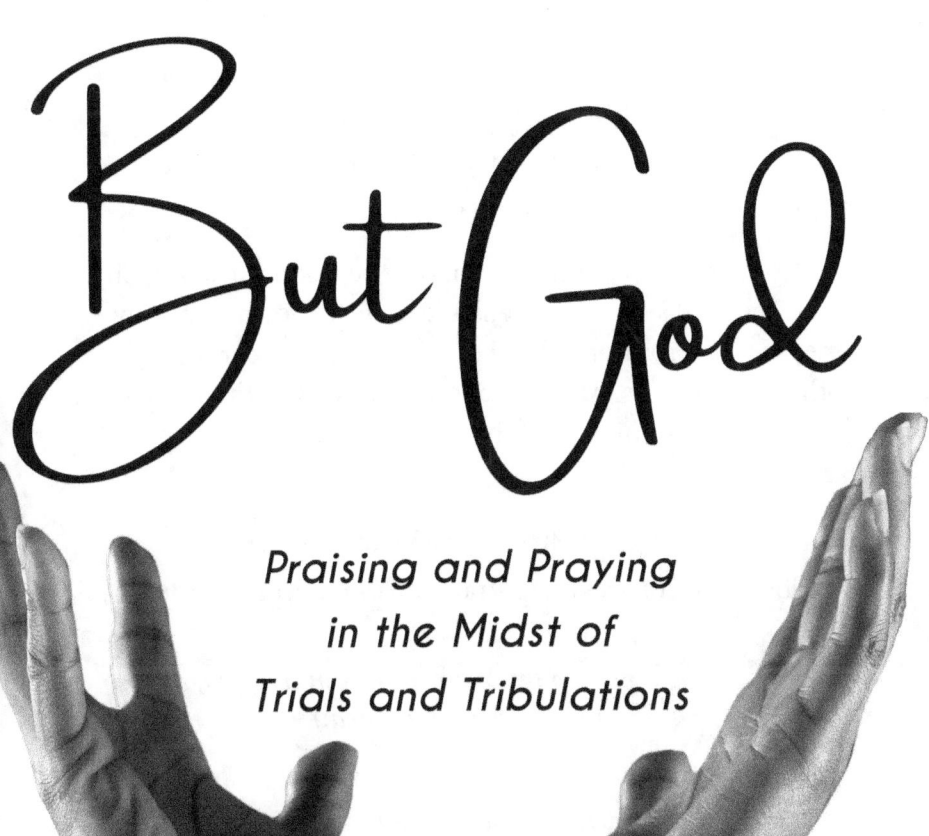

But God

Praising and Praying in the Midst of Trials and Tribulations

ALICIA E. CEASER

ISBN: 978-1-955622-13-4

Library of Congress Registration Number: TXu 2-336-461

(The names in this book have been changed, unless otherwise stated.)

Cover Art: iStock.com/Juanmonino

Published by

Fideli Publishing, Inc.
119 W. Morgan St.
Martinsville, IN 46151

www.FideliPublishing.com